THE GOOSE

JOHN

HUSS

THE GOOSE

LUKE WALKER

Truth is the last conqueror.

John Huss

WRATH AND GRACE
PUBLISHING

ACKNOWLEDGMENTS

Thank you to my editing team, Brady Erickson, Nick Larson, Zach Larson, Carlos Gonzalez, Omri Miles, and Franky Collozo. Thank you to Johan Henao for the privilege of working for Wrath and Grace. Thank you especially to my dear wife Angel for all her patience and support and wisdom and help. I love you! No thanks would be complete without mention of my dear beloved flock at Redeeming Cross and my co-elder Gottfried Caspari and all of his support in the ministry.

Soli Deo Gloria!

To the memory of
My dear friends, the Pals:

Jamison, Kathryne,
Ezra, Violet, and Calvin

Til we meet again in sweeter realms

INTRODUCTION

I am a steward of the things in this little book. There is nothing original here. Seeking to catch a fresh glance at very old things, I have steeped myself in the lore—and I use that word in the proper sense of a body of tradition and knowledge, not of legend and myth—the *lore*, I say, as it exists among the finest of Protestant historians. I add nothing of my own but a linguistic flourish here and there. The aim remains the same as in my other historical works: to whet the popular appetite for the treasures of church history.

The Reformation of the sixteenth century was an epoch in history, and, forgotten as it is, we can never be thankful enough to live on this side of it. In the end, we must remember that it was nothing more than a drive back to what the inspired writer of Hebrews calls "the time of reformation,"[1] for that is the nickname he gives to Christ's coming and the full revelation of the gospel. The real glory of the Reformation of the sixteenth century was that it was a handmaiden to lead men back to the apostolic truths of the first age.

The tragedy which follows was in truth the death knell of the popish infallibility. "No pope or ecumenical synod since has made any apology for it... So long as the dogmas of an infallible Church

[1] Hebrews 9:10.

organization and an infallible pope continue to be strictly held, no apology can be expected… Luther, in his *Address to the German Nobility*, called upon the Roman Church to confess it had done wrong in burning Huss. That innocent man's blood still cries from the ground."[1]

As the 500th anniversary of the Reformation approaches, if I am able in any measure to bring the stunning life and death of Master John Huss to life for my readers, I am satisfied.

Luke Walker
September, 2017
Richfield, MN

[1] David Schaff, *History of the Christian Church: 5.2 The Middle Ages: A.D. 1294-1517* (New York: Charles Scribner's Sons, 1920), 5.2.383.

JOHN HUSS
THE GOOSE

The ashes of John Wycliffe have been spread abroad by the currents of the high seas. His body thus dispersed, his doctrine has likewise been scattered. Though the great champion is no more, the morning star of truth has fairly arisen and the light of Christ is shining. "Let us cast our eyes over wide Christendom. What do we see? Lo! yonder in the far-off East is the same preparatory process begun which we have already traced in England. Verily, the Husbandman is wisely busy."[1] Bohemia shall be his next field. The torch of truth is to be passed once more before the great dawn of the Reformation; a goose shall squawk before the swan sings.

We find ourselves in the ancient city of Prague on the brooks of the Vltava River, and it is here that we will trace the steps of another Reformer before the Reformation. Wycliffe and Huss have been called such, as they appeared ahead of time to prepare the way.[2] We will add John Huss to that great cloud of witnesses that have come before us; may we mimic his faith in following the Lord Jesus Christ. John

---

[1] James A. Wylie, *The History of Protestantism* (London: Cassell Petter & Galpin, 1899), 1.130.

[2] David Schaff, *History of the Christian Church: 5.2 The Middle Ages: A.D. 1294-1517* (New York: Charles Scribner's Sons, 1920), 5.2.314.

Wycliffe is called the morning star of the Reformation; John Huss was, "if we may be allowed the expression, the John-Baptist of the Reformation."[1] The name is not unfitting, for he was most certainly "a burning and shining lamp,"[2] as we will see before the end.

GOOSELAND

Let us commence with a glance at the history of the church in Bohemia. The church here tended toward Greek Orthodoxy, which means that, as opposed to the Roman Catholic liturgy, the services were conducted in the language of the people rather than in Latin. It also means that the people were in the habit of taking the Lord's Supper in both kinds.[3] This Orthodox bent lent itself to a freer air in Bohemia, although the worship was eventually reduced to Roman control.[4]

Many Waldensian Christians, from that ancient church hid in the Alps of Northern Italy, had fled for safety to Bohemia. It is even rumored that Peter

---

[1] JH Merle d'Aubigné, *History of the Reformation* (New York: American Tract Society, 1849), 1.92.

[2] John 5:35.

[3] The bread and the cup.

[4] *The John the Baptist of the Reformation* (Birmingham: Solid Ground Christian Books, 2013), 3.

Waldo himself was there for a time.[1] "All through the fourteenth century, these Waldensian exiles continued to sow the seed of a pure Christianity in the soil of Bohemia."[2] God was preserving his church for a time of awakening.

Huss himself was not without forerunners of his own. When great men appear alone upon the stage, they are ever found to be part of the network of saints leading back into the depths of church history, even to the very roots of Mount Zion. One of these golden links in the chain of Bohemian history is John Milicius, a learned and mighty preacher. He went to Rome and, upon seeing the rampant immorality in the capital, wrote the following words above a Cardinal's door, "Antichrist is now come, and sitteth in the Church."[3] He escaped untouched, though not unsought. A papal bull from Gregory XI followed him to Bohemia, but the archbishop failed to execute it for fear of revolt among his glad hearers.[4]

Another, named Matthew Janovius, preached salvation by faith alone in Christ alone and "thundered in the pulpit...against the abuses of the Church."[5] Persecution broke forth. As he died he

---

[1] Wylie, *History*, 1.131.
[2] Ibid.
[3] Ibid., 1.132.
[4] Ibid., 1.132-33.
[5] Ibid., 1.133.

told his disciples, "The rage of the enemies of the truth now prevails against us, but it will not be for ever; there shall arise one from among the common people, without sword or authority, and against him they will not be able to prevail."[1] The Lord, it seems, was unwilling to leave his little flock without hopeful presentiments of the coming of greater champions.

THE GOSLING

John Huss was born on July 6, 1373, in a town called Hussinetz, from which he was named *Huss.*[2] In that tongue the word means *goose*, and, as Dickens might have it, "This must be distinctly understood, or nothing wonderful can come of the story I am going to relate."[3] His father died when he was young. After basic education, his mother took him to Prague, where there stood a prestigious school, "the first of the German universities."[4] As she did so, she asked God's blessing on the young man. "The prayers of the mother," says a quillman, "were heard, though the answer came in a way that would have pierced her heart like a sword, had she lived to witness the issue."[5]

---

[1] Ibid., 1.133.

[2] Ibid., 1.134.

[3] Charles Dickens, *A Christmas Carol* (London: J.M. Dent & Sons, 1907), 9.

[4] Schaff, *History*, 5.2.359.

[5] Wylie, *History*, 1.134.

Upon graduation, he became a distinguished professor at the University of Prague. It was here that, as providence would have it, the young gosling had a lethal encounter with the writings of John Wycliffe. His friend Jerome had brought the spiritual outlaw's books from England to Prague in the year 1400. He may have even encountered them sooner. "Wyclif's views and writings were known in Bohemia at an early date," as early as 1391.[1] In any case, the breach had been made; the Lutterworth preacher yet speaks from beyond the grave.

Providence played its ever-marching role in these matters. The King's sister, named Anne, was married to Richard II of England.[2] There she became a disciple of John Wycliffe through his writings. When she died, her servants brought her Wycliffe contraband back to Bohemia.[3] The hand of God was driving the Wycliffite doctrine deep into Europe. "The spiritually dead who are in their graves were beginning to hear the voice of Wicliffe—yea, rather of Christ speaking through Wicliffe—and to come forth."[4]

---

[1] Schaff, *History*, 5.2.360.
[2] Ibid., 5.2.359.
[3] Wylie, *History*, 1.135.
[4] Ibid., 1.130.

THE GOOSE BEGINS TO HONK

"The true career of John Huss dates from about A.D. 1402, when he was appointed preacher to the Chapel of Bethlehem."[1] After becoming a professor, he entered the ministry; "his sermons formed an epoch in Prague."[2] As he preached, he was gripped by the truth of the gospel, and was sometime during this course converted. He steeped his soul in the writings of Wycliffe[3] and those of more, shall we say, *inspired* men; he came face to face with the gospel of salvation through Christ alone. Learned men see him reading Wycliffe's works and remark that the cursed author is in hell; look how Huss owns the affiliation: "I only wish that my soul, when it leaves this body, may reach the place where that of this excellent Briton now dwells."[4] In time he was to realize, if this is what it means to be a Wycliffite, then there was nothing for it. A Wycliffite he was. Little did he know—or did he?—that after he finished his course, a greater than Wycliffe was destined to adopt the name of *Hussite*.

As to his preaching, the people heard him gladly. He was given a generous measure of eloquence, a

---

[1] Ibid., 1.134.
[2] Ibid., 1.134.
[3] "As early as 1402, Huss was regarded as the chief exponent and defender of Wycliffian views at the university." Schaff, 5.2.361.
[4] *John the Baptist*, 5-6.

sonorous honk, if you like. What's more, he preached the free grace of God, which is eloquence itself to the sinner's heart. It was a breath of fresh air in the ancient land. Through their new herald, "Wyclif's writings were sown broadcast in Bohemia."[1] The English heresy spread like wildfire in Prague through every strata of society as the people hung upon every word of this extraordinary preacher. Already, it seems, he was "famous among all the churches for his preaching of the gospel."[2] "In the midst of this sunken community stood up Huss, like an incarnate conscience,"[3] and he "touched the sensitive feelings of the monks,"[4] as he preached against their abuses.

Naturally, this eloquent preacher did not go unanswered. The words of Paul ever follow the preaching of the gospel: "There are many adversaries."[5] He was attacked by Rome; they were most decidedly not *down* with this Goose. Papal bulls assaulted him, but he valued them at a feather's weight. What fine kindling Papal Bulls make is yet to be seen in our studies. He was commanded not to preach in the language of the people and not to preach the doctrines of Wycliffe, yet he continued fearlessly to

---

[1] Schaff, *History*, 5.2.362.

[2] 2 Cor. 8:18.

[3] Wylie, 1.135.

[4] Georg Lommel, *John Huss; A Memoir* (London: R.B. Seeley and W. Burnside, 1841), 27.

[5] 1 Cor. 16:9.

do so. The mark upon the man Huss is courage. He preached the gospel come hell or high water.

Eventually, the archbishop gathered all of the heretical books he could find in Prague—including the works of Wycliffe, Huss, and Jerome—and burned 200 of them in his palace.[1] Such had become Wycliffe's following, that some of these handwritten books (the printing press was not as yet invented) were beautifully bound and set with gems.[2] Though dead, Wycliffe was yet gathering disciples from the wealthiest to the poorest of society. The gospel marched through the people with dignified, lordly step.

The blessed volumes reduced to ashes, riots ensued. "Huss's sermons at this time, far from calming the commotion, were adapted to increase it."[3] He was preaching raucous reform in Prague; this could not go unanswered for long. The Pope responded in kind with an unheeded summons to Rome followed by an interdict launched upon Prague.[4] John Huss was defiant before what he calls the "bolts of anti-christ."[5] He went further and "publicly asserted that the pope was exercising prerogatives

---

[1] Schaff, *History*, 5.2.363.
[2] Wylie, *History*, 1.137.
[3] Schaff, *History*, 5.2.363.
[4] Wylie, 1.137.
[5] Schaff, *History*, 5.2.367.

received from the devil."[1] At this time he declared "that he was ready to suffer a dreadful death rather than to declare what would be contrary to the will of Christ and his Church."[2]

Huss was condemned by the religious authorities in full, yet popular opinion remained on his side. The people flocked to him. Even King Wenceslaus commanded the priests, "You shall leave my goose in peace, who lays me golden eggs."[3] A university student and a shoemaker named Stasseck stood up to the leaders of the synagogue, the student going so far as to say, "Now is it plain that the Pope is truly Antichrist, since he has proclaimed a crusade against Christians."[4] The tide was rising, and in these two individuals Bohemia was given its first martyrs. No man could halt the movement now. However, in submission to the king's wishes, Huss decided to leave Prague in hopes of lifting the interdict off of the city, for its own sake.[5]

---

[1] Ibid., 5.2.366.
[2] Ibid., 5.2.364.
[3] *John the Baptist*, 8.
[4] Ibid., 17.
[5] Schaff, *History*, 5.2.366.

THE GOOSE SPREADS HIS WINGS

With Prague behind him, Huss returned to his homeland and preached through towns and villages. "The Church," said his eager new hearers, "has pronounced this man a heretic and a demon, yet his life is holy, and his doctrine is pure and elevating."[1] He continued in the esteem of the people and of the nobility; "lords in their strong castles protected him."[2]

In this period of exile, he began to wrestle further with the truth. The Roman Catholic Church taught its own infallibility; she had received word from the Holy Spirit that she could receive word from the Holy Spirit. How very convenient. Considering the rampant sin in the camp, Huss' conscience recoiled at these claims. "If the authority was just and infallible, as he believed it to be, how came it to be that he felt compelled to disobey it? To obey, he saw, was to sin; but why should obedience to an infallible church lead to such an issue? This was the problem he could not solve; this was the doubt that tortured him hour by hour."[3] Master Wycliffe had passed almost instantly into the full-grown freedom of the gospel, throwing off the papal holds from his mind.

---

[1] Wylie, *History*, 1.137.
[2] Schaff, *History*, 5.2.366.
[3] Wylie, *History*, 1.137.

"The Bohemian preacher," on the other hand, "had appealed to the Bible, but he had not bowed before it with the absolute and unreserved submission of the English pastor."[1] John Huss struggled until the day that he died with loyalty to the hierarchy, after a fashion.[2] As he encountered the bold assertions of Wycliffe, and of the Scriptures, his soul reeled in turmoil.

By and by he began to embrace the liberating principle of *sola scriptura*. He tore down every idol of authority other than the word of God, and this is what finally resolved his difficulties. The word of God alone is where the living God speaks. Whether Huss knew it or not, there was no turning back now. To disagree on a doctrine here or there with Rome was one thing (not an *undeadly* thing, mind you), but to disagree on this fundamental level was to strike at the very foundation and threaten the whole edifice. Such is the outcome of embracing the authority of the Bible alone. In doing so, "he committed the unpardonable sin of the Middle Ages."[3] And now, alas, "the Bohemian theologian was fully imbued with Wyclif's heretical spirit."[4] The Englishman's quill had pierced his heart.

---

[1] Ibid., 1.136.
[2] We will get to this.
[3] Schaff, *History*, 5.2.370.
[4] Ibid., 5.2.371.

He wrote while in exile. Among writings of this
period are *On the Church*, a famous book in his day,
and *The Six Errors,* which exposed the abuses of the
popes, bishops, cardinals, and priests. He uttered
portentous words during this time as well:

> The wicked have begun by preparing a
> treacherous snare for the goose. But if even
> the goose, which is only a domestic bird, a
> peaceful animal, and whose flight is not very
> high in the air, has nevertheless broken
> through their toils, other birds, soaring more
> boldly towards the sky, will break through
> them with still greater force. Instead of a
> feeble goose, the truth will send forth eagles
> and keen-eyed vultures.[1]

We must note one more matter before we come
to the rub in Huss's life, and that is the Papal Schism.
My faithful readership will recall from Wycliffe that
the so-called successor of Peter had grown multiple
heads at this juncture. There were competing popes
and the apostolic succession became altogether un-
clear as men grasped for the triple crown and hurled
anathemas at one another. In Wycliffe's day there
were two, in Huss', three.[2]

---

[1] d'Aubigné, *History,* 1.92-3.
[2] Wylie, *History,* 1.142.

The fact of the schism suggested some difficulties for the doctrine of infallibility:

"If we must obey," said Huss and his followers, "to whom is our obedience to be paid? Balthazar Cossa, called John XXIII., is at Bologna; Angelo Corario, named Gregory XII., is at Rimini; Peter de Lune, who calls himself Benedict XIII., is in Arragon. If all three are infallible, why doesn't their testimony agree? And if only one of them is the most holy father, why is it we can't distinguish him from the rest?" Nor was much help to be got towards a solution by putting the question to the men themselves. If they asked John XXIII., he told them Gregory XII. was "a heretic, a demon, the Antichrist;" Gregory XII. obligingly bore the same testimony about John XXIII. And both Gregory and John united in sounding in similar fashion the praises of Benedict XIII., whom they stigmatized as "an imposter and schismatic," while Benedict paid back with prodigal interest the compliments of his two opponents. It came to this, that if these men were to be believed, instead of three Popes there were three Antichrists in Christendom; and if they were not to be believed, where

was the infallibility, and what had become of
the apostolic succession?[1]

Reasonable thoughts; yea, impossible to refute.

These popes (the pope is ever legion) launched
crusades against each other, like the crusades into
Palestine. Indulgences were held before the people
to encourage their holy zeal. John XXIII "promised
to all who should join the crusade," (professing
Christian soldiers sent to slaughter other Christian
soldiers), "or who should preach it, or collect funds
for its support, the pardon of all their sins, and
immediate admission into Paradise should they die in
the war—in short, the same indulgences which were
accorded to those who bore arms for the conquest
of the Holy Land."[2] At these words the thoughtful
reader may well ask, Is this the doctrine of Mecca or
of Rome? There remains an unhappy confusion of
dogma there. For they are, after all, sister systems,
various manifestations of that cursed, iron-fisted
theocracy which seeks to rule the consciences of men
with physical threats and wispy promises.

This was not an unattractive offer to poor souls
in the darkened day of which we speak. The people
did not believe—for it was not taught to them—that
their sins could be forgiven in full, nor that they

---

[1] Ibid., 1.141.
[2] Ibid., 1.142.

could have assurance of such a magnificent trans-
action, were it even to take place. What's more, they
believed they were headed for purgatory after death.
To such people, *holy war* held great promise, and it
continues to do so for desperate souls today. Wonder
of wonders, this is precisely the promise of the
gospel: full pardon, assurance of forgiveness, and
immediate reception into the paradise of God at
death. Satan has truly blinded the minds of un-
believers to keep them from seeing the light of the
gospel of the glory of Christ.

As to the pope, Huss says "if he abuses his power
by enjoining what is contrary to the Divine Law, then
it is a duty to resist him as should be done to the pale
horse of the Apocalypse, to the dragon, to the beast,
and to the Leviathan."[1] The poor were ever trampled
by the religious powers that be. "They array the
bones of the [saints] with silk and gold and silver, and
lodge them magnificently; but they refuse clothing
and hospitality to the poor members of Jesus Christ
who are amongst us, at whose expense they feed to
repletion, and drink till they are intoxicated."[2] What
is more, John XXIII was selling pardon in exchange
for the spilling of Christian blood, all to protect his
own neck. Huss was already warm; "the persecutions

---

[1] Ibid., 1.142.
[2] Ibid., 1.143

which he endured may have heated his temper."[1] He now saw further atrocities and "it was not easy to witness all this and be calm."[2] Huss was heated! How very *heated* he was to become in the great cause of the ages, we shall soon discover.

THE COUNCIL OF QUACKS

Much is in motion to disrupt Christendom. The Goose's *foul* teaching is overturning Bohemia; three popes are cursing each other from their thrones. What is to be done? The newly crowned emperor Sigismund now decided to call a General Council at Constance to deal with these pressing matters. "These were the two objects which the emperor had in eye—to heal the schism and to extirpate heresy."[3] Huss was summoned, and wrote to his dear flock, looking to God "that I may not shrink from the Gospel, but be more and more enlightened by its clear and sanctifying truth—that I may extirpate the doctrines of Antichrist, and leave a bright example for the imitation of my brethren."[4] The prayer was not unheard.

---

[1] Ibid.
[2] Ibid.
[3] Ibid., 1.146.
[4] *John the Baptist*, 28.

He went to the council by choice. "I came here of my own free will. If I had been unwilling to come, neither that king nor this king here would have been able to force me to come, so numerous and so powerful are the Bohemian nobles who love me, and within whose castles I should have been able to lie concealed."[1] No one took his life from him; in a figure, he laid it down of his own accord. Lords most heartily defended the people's champ—"this darling of the people," as one calls him.[2] In addition, King Wenceslaus furnished him with "two staunch knights, the lords of Chlum and Lestna, as companions and protectors."[3] The former, John of Chlum, testifies to the general support of Huss among the nobility: "There are numbers of great nobles who love him and have strong castles where they could keep him as long as they wished, even against both those kings."[4] With a clear path of retreat open to him, Huss went of his own volition through the gates of deep darkness. He was Christian liberty at its finest. "Conscious of his innocence and the justice of his cause, thither he went."[5]

---

[1] Schaff, *History*, 5.2.367.
[2] *John the Baptist*, 11.
[3] Ibid., 25.
[4] Schaff, *History*, 5.2.367.
[5] Wylie, *History*, 1.148.

People flocked to Constance from all over Europe; the city swelled to about 100,000 during the council.[1] A great gathering no doubt, but paling in comparison to our cities of ten millions plus. This was the highest platform that age could afford. In the technological age in which we find ourselves, we must all of us be ready to bear witness upon the most prominent stages the world has ever seen.

As to churchmen, "Thirty cardinals, twenty archbishops, one hundred and fifty bishops, and as many prelates, a multitude of abbots and doctors, and eighteen hundred priests came together in obedience to the joint summons of the emperor and the Pope."[2] Among these vast clerical convoys, a contrast presents itself to us, too bold to ignore. In their midst is a tale of two Johns; it was the best of Johns and the worst of Johns.

John Huss, having no earthly power, arrives with a mere 8 persons (the number of righteous on the earth has been limited to this digit before). From town to town he is greeted with love and support, and goes on with resolve. He "expected to find more enemies at the Council than Jesus Christ had at Jerusalem."[3] And yet his steps are marked by the energy of a clean conscience and the mettle of one

---

[1] Ibid., 1.147.
[2] Ibid., 1.146.
[3] Ibid., 1.148.

whose hope resides beyond the pale of this passing world. He posted letters in the city squares through which he passed, stating, "Maister Iohn Hus is ready to satisfie euery man at the said councel which shal lay any thing vnto his charge as touchig his faith."[1] Though he go to an apostate Jerusalem, he was showed the highest honor by magistrates and common men at every town, "his journey was a triumphal procession in a sort."[2] In fact, he testifies that "he found in no place so great ennemies as in Boheme."[3] Truly a prophet is not without honor except in his hometown. He was going on to victory, but victory of the Lord's own kind.

Another John, named by the august Roman numerals XXIII, traveled hence, attended by a strong retinue without, and assailed by a stronger conscience within. "To the Pope the idea of a Council was beyond alarming. Nor can one wonder at this, if his conscience was loaded with but half the crimes of which Popish historians have accused him."[4] He was a notorious sinner, guilty of nearly every abomination. He probably poisoned the man before him so that he could wear the holy garments. He gave

---

[1] John Foxe, *The Unabridged Acts and Monuments Online or TAMO* (1575 edition) (HRI Online Publications, Sheffield, 2011), 2.248. Available from: http://www.johnfoxe.org [Accessed: 09.05.17].

[2] Wylie, *History*, 1.148.

[3] Foxe, *Acts*, 2.248.

[4] Wylie, *History*, 1.146.

gifts along the way to Constance, in the hope of securing a safe retreat if perchance his ominous presentiments were borne out in waking life. He knows that he will be called to account. Earthly power and wealth at his fingertips, but he cannot escape.

Here we have a royal John and a beggar John, and their outward appearance could not have been more squarely contrary to the truth. The men who bore them were in reality inverted, a sort of negative image. For "what is exalted among men is an abomination in the sight of God."[1]

As John Huss traveled to Constance, he held in his possession a significant document. The Holy Roman Emperor, Sigusmund, had given to him an imperial safe-conduct for his journey. I will take the liberty to quote the document at length:

> To all ecclesiastical and secular princes, &c., and to all our subjects,
>
> We recommend to you with a full affection, to all in general and to each in particular, the honourable Master John Huss, Bachelor in Divinity, and Master of Arts, the bearer of these presents, journeying from Bohemia to

---

[1] Luke 16:15.

the Council of Constance, whom we have taken under our protection and safeguard, and under that of the Empire, enjoining you to receive him and treat him kindly, furnishing him with all that shall be necessary to speed and assure his journey, as well by water as by land, without taking anything from him or his at coming in or going out, for any sort of duties whatsoever; and calling on you to allow him to pass, sojourn, stop, and return freely and securely, providing him even, if necessary, with good passports, for the honour and respect of the Imperial Majesty.

Given at Spires this 18th day of October of the year 1414, the third of our reign in Hungary, and the fifth of that of the Romans.[1]

Encouraged, as Foxe has it, by "so many fayre promises,"[2] Huss proceeded to Constance. This was no scrap parchment. It was an oath written in blood, a guarantee of safe passage from the highest earthly

---

[1] Wylie, *History*, 1.154; *John the Baptist*, 25-6 in full.
[2] Foxe, *Acts*, 2.244.

power. "How that pledge was redeemed," says one, "we shall see by-and-by."[1]

When he arrived, he was promptly questioned. "For this cause," he replied, "am I come to the council, that my errors may be pointed out to me, and that with sorrow and contrition of heart I may renounce them."[2] And yet he knew his strength, "I came here to speak in open council according to the ability, which I trust God will not withhold from me."[3] Such bold humility was a shock to the churchmen gathered in Constance, one which perhaps their eyes had never witnessed in flesh and blood. Thus we see the rare character of godly men of all ages, men who ever seek to subject their very selves to the word of God, and refuse to move an inch before any lesser authority. The spirit of the Reformers was a peacemaking one which made efforts to reform the church from within. It was their enemies who threw down the gage and drew the line in the sand; it was Rome that finally cast them out of the synagogue.

One of the first judgments of the council was swift in its execution:

In the eighth session (May 4th, 1415), John Wicliffe was summoned from his rest, cited

---

[1] Wylie, *History*, 1.154.
[2] Lommel, *Huss*, 61-2.
[3] *John the Baptist*, 37.

before the Council, and made answerable to
it for his moral writings. Forty-five prop-
ositions, previously culled from his publications, were condemned, and this sentence
was fittingly followed by a decree consigning
their author to the flames. Wicliffe himself
being beyond their reach, his bones, pursuant
to this sentence, were afterwards dug up and
burned.[1]

Lest the bones of the prophet should do any further
quickening, they must be destroyed!

The deposition of John XXIII followed hard by.
He fled from Constance in disguise.[2] He was resisted
even by the emperor, "and the Council, seconding
Sigismund with its spiritual weapons, wrested the
infallibility from the Pope, and took that formidable
engine into its own hands."[3] The Council was now
almighty. The renegade pope returned in shame to
Constance and, as providence would have it, was
thrown into the same prison then inhabited by our
other John. Schaff is too delicate when he says, "it
was a strange freak of history."[4] It was, we dare not
doubt, a matter of God's stunning providence.

---

[1] Wylie, *History*, 1.149-51.

[2] Ibid., 1.152.

[3] Ibid.

[4] Schaff, *History*, 5.2.375.

Wylie, that prince of Protestant historians, sees in the Council's condemnation of John XXIII its own condemnation. We will hear him in his own words:

Before turning to the more tragic page of the history of the Council, we have to remark that it seems almost as if the Fathers at Constance were intent on erecting beforehand a monument to the innocence of John Huss, and to their own guilt in the terrible fate to which they were about to consign him. The crimes for which they condemned Balthazar Cossa, John XXIII., were the same, only more atrocious and fouler, as those of which Huss accused the priesthood, and for which he demanded a reformation. The condemnation of Pope John was, therefore, whether the Council confessed it or not, the vindication of Huss. "When all the members of the Council shall be scattered in the world like storks," said Huss, in a letter which he wrote to a friend at this time, "they will know when winter cometh what they did in summer."[1]

---

[1] Wylie, *History*, 1.153.

THE GOOSE IN HOT WATER

We shall now turn to this more tragic page. Within a month at Constance he was apprehended. His enemies had "trotted vp & down, hether and thether, taking great paines"[1] to prejudice the hierarchy's view of Huss. "On the twenty-sixth day after his arrival Huss was arrested, in flagrant violation of the imperial safe-conduct, and carried before the Pope and the cardinals."[2] The emperor had not yet arrived, but the priests seized and placed him in a monastery dungeon by the river. "Preparations had been going on for several days to provide the place with locks, bolts and other strong furnishings."[3] Fortified armaments against a peaceful preacher the world had seen before.[4] The sewage from the monastery flowed out close to his cell. Truly, this was a man of whom the world was not worthy.

He withered here for three months. He was given no advocate—though his Advocate dwelt on high. No doctor is sent to his cell—though the great Physician himself was his personal attendant. The imperial safe-conduct is being violated—though

---

[1] Foxe, *Acts*, 2.249.
[2] Wylie, *History*, 1.154.
[3] Schaff, *History*, 5.2.373.
[4] Luke 22:52.

God's promises are sure as ever. "Christ deceives no man by a safe-conduct," he reflected. "What he pledges he fulfills."[1] When the emperor finally did arrive, the infallible Council had its way with him. He was swayed not to keep faith with a heretic, and that promises to such a one could in fact be broken. As to the matter of keeping one's word, "Luther declared that a safe-conduct promised to the devil must be kept."[2]

Huss brushed with death in his dungeon quarters; eventually doctors were sent. The priests did not wish to lose their prey, such holy men were they. For they knew in their minds what they wanted to do with him. He was relocated to a prison with better air, but there, never too comfy, he was weighed with heavy chains. During the day he was free to walk about his cell, but at night they fastened him to the wall "hard by his bed."[3]

Seven months passed before he appeared before the council even once. "Individual liberty had no rights before the bar of an ecclesiastical court in the 15th century when a heretic was under accusation."[4] And yet he retained his fortitude against all ecclesiastical intimidation. Spying what lay at the end

---

[1] Schaff, *History*, 5.2.385.

[2] Ibid., 5.2.386.

[3] Foxe, *Acts*, 2.253.

[4] Schaff, *History*, 5.2.373.

of such a course, he says, "I trust in my lord Iesus, that he wil so comfort & strengthen me, that I shall desiremuch rather to die for his glory sake."[1]

He wrote many letters during this time, for "his faithful companion Chlum, vanquishing all hitherto insurmountable difficulties, found means to furnish him with pen, ink, paper, and a Bible."[2] Four main themes present themselves in these correspondences: "Huss' reliance upon the king and his word of honor, his consuming desire to be heard in open council, the expectation of possible death and his trust in God."[3]

Truth ever seeks release as it burns in the bones of God's men in their appointed hours. Master Huss desired open Bibles and open discussion. Had not all the doctors of the church gathered for just this very thing? He sought it fiercely. It is not exactly right to speak of him feeling his own strength; it is better to say that he felt the strength of the truth within him and he wished to unleash it upon men's consciences.

He appeared before the council three times. The first was on June 5th, 1415. What sermon prep he had—six months of wasting away in filthy prisons— will make the cowardly conduct of his foes all the

---

[1] Foxe, *Acts*, 2.249.

[2] *John the Baptist*, 52.

[3] Schaff, *History*, 5.2.375.

more conspicuous. They strove to delay his appearance, for they "feared the effect of his eloquence upon the members."[1] Whether conscious of it, or whether it lurked at the back of their darkened minds, the divine promise had suited itself to such a one as Huss: "I will give you a mouth and wisdom, which none of your adversaries will be able to withstand or contradict."[2] This is what they feared.

A case was built against him prior to his summons and presented in writing to the Pope. The articles, divided by broad category of error, were marshaled to secure Huss's condemnation. Lo! the Romish preachers could reach, as well as the Reverend Haynes, unto the majestic heights of the *seventhly* and *eighthly* in their orations. And in their case it was not without, after their own fashion, thoughts that "richly rewarded the attention of the hearers,"[3] Pope John XXIII and his court. In these divisions, Huss was accused of such things as administering the Lord's Supper to the people in both kinds, rejecting the transubstantiation—which he most explicitly denied rejecting—and denouncing the hierarchy as such and instead recognizing only the authority of godly priests.[4] They read these charges to him in his

---

[1] Wylie, *History*, 1.155.
[2] Luke 21:15.
[3] Timothy Mather Cooley, *Sketches of the Life and Character of the Rev. Lemuel Haynes* (New York: John S. Taylor, 1839), 293.
[4] Foxe, *Acts*, 2.251-53.

prison; he requested an advocate to speak for him, but was denied.

Many charges were brought against him upon his appearance, some false—"I am accused," he says, "of errors which I have never taught nor believed; how then can I renounce them?"—and some true—"How, on the other hand, can I give up doctrines which I have taught in full belief of their truth, until I have been convinced of their fallacy?"[1] They placed his books before the council; the author owned them as his own and sought to make some reply to the accusations. "He had not uttered more than a few words when there arose in the hall a clamour so loud as completely to drown his voice... He had not gone far till he had occasion to appeal to the Scriptures; the storm was that moment renewed, with greater violence than before."[2] Some laughed while others roared. Is it any wonder? "If a wise man has an argument with a fool, the fool only rages and laughs, and there is no quiet."[3] At all costs, the Goose must not speak. His darts were too well feathered. How terrified of the Scriptures were these masters of the church!

---

[1] *John the Baptist*, 78.
[2] Wylie, *History*, 1.156-58.
[3] Proverbs 29:9.

"Art thou wiser than a whole council?" asked his
foes in private at a later occasion. "No," he said,
"send the least of your members here, that he may
instruct me from the Scriptures."[1] This request won
him the title of *obstinate heretic*. One, himself not un-
acquainted with the mindless ragings of ravenous
foes, has reflected on the situation before us thusly:
"All worked themselves into rage like wild boars; the
bristles of their back stood on end, they bent their
brows and gnashed their teeth against John Huss."[2]
It was "an exhibition of contempt which the em-
barrassed Emperor in vain endeavored to check."[3]
The meeting was disbanded without a defense from
the accused.

Two days later the Council reconvened. That
morning, June 7th, saw a solar eclipse.[4] The Council
dared not continue while the omen lasted. The light
returned, and now Huss and Sigismund meet in
person. He looked, finally, into the face of the man
who had guaranteed the safety of his person. "The
irons that Huss wore were a strange commentary,
truly, on the imperial safe-conduct."[5] Although Sigismund may have resolved to wash his own hands,

---

[1] *John the Baptist*, 91.
[2] Martin Luther, quoted in Wylie, *History*, 1.158.
[3] *John the Baptist*, 70.
[4] NASA confirms this, https://eclipse.gsfc.nasa.gov/SEcat5/SE1401-
1500.html. The council's findings on a flat-earth are unknown to the author.
[5] Wylie, *History*, 1.158.

and was even "from selfish motives, anxious for the liberation of Huss,"[1] he was nevertheless carried away before the Council, till "the imperial safe-conduct and the martyr's stake had taken their place, side by side, ineffaceably, on the history's eternal page."[2]

Huss refused to budge. The infallible council, feeling its own strength, demanded absolute submission from the poor priest who stood before it. They didn't want to reason about specifics; all they wanted was wholesale recantation and blind submission. A doctor among them went so far as to say, "If the Council should even tell you that you have but one eye, you would be obliged to agree with the Council."[3] He refused to submit to any such tyranny of the conscience. All they asked was, as it were, but a pinch of incense offered before their infallibility. After all, they had just deposed the pope himself; what was it then for them to require full submission from the Bohemian? And yet he holds his ground. His soul was of tougher stuff than iron.

Huss' primary offense was the preaching of Scripture alone. This was his canon and he required that his opponents convince according to its rule; apart from that he would not give way before them.

---

[1] *John the Baptist*, 83.
[2] Wylie, *History*, 1.158.
[3] Ibid., 1.160.

He also preached that the true church was the elect. The Roman Catholic Church asserted that the hierarchy itself was the church, but not the people. Huss affirmed against the Papacy that the people of God were the church. He also preached the sovereignty of God in salvation and the equality of bishops. The pope was nothing more than a normal bishop; only, he happened to be the bishop of Rome. These were high crimes in that tyrannical age.

He also attacked the crusades and the indulgences. "God alone possesses the power to forgive sins in an absolute manner."[1] The indulgences—whence forgiveness could be bought with money, or *simony*, he outright condemned. Rome yet proffers indulgences from time to time in our own day. In fact, an indulgence to shave time off purgatory was recently offered to everyone who followed the Pope on Twitter.[2]

How sweet the tweet, that saved a wretch like me.

In contradistinction from @Pontifex, Master Huss—whilst exceeding the customary 140 characters—wrote his flock back in Prague: "I commend you to the merciful Lord Jesus Christ our true God,

---

[1] Ibid., 1.142.
[2] https://www.theatlantic.com/international/archive/2013/07/what-the-pope-really-meant-in-his-twitter-indulgences-announcement/277909.

and to the Son of the immaculate virgin Mary, who has redeemed us by his most bitter death, without all of our merits, from eternal pains, from the thralldom of the devil and from sin."[1] Towards his death he says, "I would not for a chapel full of gold recede from the truth. The truth stands and is mighty forever. In the truth of the gospel I have written, taught, preached, and today I will gladly die in it."[2] In the end, "he had transferred his allegiance from the Church to God speaking in his word. This was his great crime... He had rent from his conscience the shackles of the infallibility."[3]

An Englishmen by the name of John Stokes was present at the council. He was a fierce opponent of Wycliffe and had strode across the Continent to witness the festivities. "It seemed to him as if he saw Wyclif himself in bodily form sitting before him,"[4] with such likeness did the disciple resemble the teacher. They were one. Their resemblance was not so much the one to the other, but both to their Master. They were like *him*, and that is why they mirrored each other.

As he left the council on that second of his appearances, June 7th, one lone soul extended a hand

---

[1] Wylie, *History*, 1.159.

[2] Ibid.

[3] Ibid.

[4] Schaff, *History*, 5.2.376.

in fraternal solidarity to the prisoner. It was his true
friend, the Lord Chlum. "Noble Professor," he ad-
ded to his gesture, "sacrifice thy life sooner than
abandon the truth."[1] The Lord ever has his Lord
Chlums and, as will be seen, his Elector Fredericks.[2]
May he send more. What an encouragement this was
to Huss in the midst of the crucible. And yet the
waves rolled over him: "That night, as Huss wrote,
he suffered from toothache, vomiting, headache and
the stone."[3] The next day, charges against him and
corresponding passages from his writings were
publicly read. "When they came to the passage that
no heretic should be put to death, the audience
shouted in mockery."[4] Their common purpose was
no longer hidden. It is one which we were warned
against long ago: "Let us lie in wait for blood."[5]

Even Sigismund, behind closed doors, tried to
summon a retractation from Huss. He did not wish
to break the safe conduct if it could be helped; and
yet, greater interests governed him. It seems to the
reader of history that Pilate was once again, though

---

[1] *John the Baptist*, 73.
[2] Two others are worthy of mention, the Bishop of Ostia and Chancellor of
the Emperor Caspar Schick, who protested the bloodthirsty council. *John the
Baptist*, 86, 97.
[3] Schaff, *History*, 5.2.377.
[4] Ibid.
[5] Prov. 1:11.

in strange and distant lands and under a different veneer, yet acting his part on the stage of history.

Well, John Huss now knew that his fate was sealed. He accepted the fact that he was going to die, and he had a pretty good idea of the method. "From that moment Huss had peace—deeper and more ecstatic than he had ever before experienced."[1] He began to charge his friends to meet him on the Other Side. "When, with the assistance of Jesus Christ, we shall meet again in the delicious peace of the future life, you will learn how merciful God has shown himself towards me—how effectually he has supported me in the midst of my temptations and trials."[2] He resigned all the conflict of the council and his defense; the *witness* now "calmly began to prepare for death, not disquieted by the terrible form in which he foresaw it would come."[3] "He was setting his house in order."[4] He resolved himself with the faith of martyrs, whose blood is ever the seed of the church, and with happy thoughts of gospel advancement. "After I have ceased to live it will be still better shown forth, by mightier preachers, to the great satisfaction of the people, and to my own most sincere joy, when I shall be again permitted to

---

[1] Wylie, *History*, 1.160.

[2] Ibid.

[3] Ibid.

[4] Schaff, *History*, 5.2.379.

announce his Gospel—that is, when I shall rise from the dead."[1]

THE GOOSE AND THE GANDER

We shall now compare Huss and Wycliffe side by side. "The council coupled the two names... Invectives flying about in Constance joined their names together."[2] How do they compare? "In honest zeal for the cause of God and Jesus Christ, both men—Wicliffe and Huss—stand on the same footing. Only in Wicliffe's case the zeal was of a more fiery, manly, energetic kind, whilst in Huss it burned with a warm, silent glow, in union with almost feminine tenderness, and fervent faith and endurance."[3] Wycliffe is the manlier, Huss the gentler specimen of champion. Indeed, "Wicliffe was a man of God, Huss was a child of God; both, however, were heroes in God's host, each according to the gifts which the Spirit of God had lent them, and in each these gifts of mind were used for the good of the whole body."[4]

---

[1] Wylie, *History*, 1.160.
[2] Schaff, *History*, 5.2.383.
[3] Lechler, quoted in Wylie, *History*, 1.166.
[4] Ibid.

As to their relation, "Wicliffe is the master, and Huss the scholar."[1] Huss did not reach the level of understanding that Wycliffe did before him, or as others did after him. For instance, it seems that he held to transubstantiation until death.[2] Wycliffe had thrown that off in a moment of lone brilliance; Huss wasn't yet free. "Even to the last he did not abandon the communion of the Roman Church."[3] Yet, he distinguished: "Huss denied the divine right of the Bishop of Rome to the primacy of the Church, and wished to restore the original equality which he held existed among the bishops of the Church. Wicliffe would have gone farther; equality among the priests and not merely among the bishops would alone have contented him.

And yet, the privileged modern reader must bear in mind that Huss was a man like us in an age very unlike our own. "It cannot be doubted that John Huss was essentially a Protestant and a Reformer."[4] The line he had taken led, whether he knew it or not, to a full separation with Rome. Just as in the case of John Owen, who's covenant theology bears implications that lead inevitably to a Baptist polity, had he lived long enough to have traced the line to its conclusion, so Huss, as he affirmed the sole authority

---

[1] Ibid, 1.165.
[2] Ibid, 1.158.
[3] Ibid.
[4] Ibid.

of the written word of God. "These, while they directly attacked certain of the principles of the Papacy, tended indirectly to the subversion of the whole system—in short, to a far greater revolution than Huss perceived, or perhaps intended."[1] It was left to another champion, likewise embarking unbeknownst on the path of reform, to follow that path to its necessary end.

As to a general comparison of the men themselves, Lechler affords us a vivid picture:

> Huss is indeed not a primitive, creative, original genius like Wicliffe, and as a thinker neither speculatively inclined nor of systematic talent. In the sphere of theological thinking Wicliffe is a kingly spirit, of an inborn power of mind, and through unwearied mental labour gained the position of a leader of thought;[2] whilst Huss appears as a star of the second magnitude, and planet-like revolves round Wicliffe as his sun. Both indeed circle round the great central Sun, which is Christ himself. Farther, Huss is not a character like Wicliffe; twice tempered and sharp as steel—an inwardly strong nature, going absolutely straight forward, without

[1] Ibid.

[2] A *thought leader*, no doubt. His TED talks were revolutionary.

looking on either side, following only his conviction, and carrying it out logically and energetically to its ultimate consequences, sometimes even with a ruggedness and harshness which wounds and repulses. In comparision with Wicliffe, Huss is a somewhat soft personality, finely strung, more receptively and passively inclined than with a vocation for independent power and heroic conquest...[1]

But Master Huss was not without his strength. What he may have lacked in knowledge, he more than made up for in courage. He paid no regard to the dangers before him; he saluted the truth of God alone. To Wycliffe was given the greater measure of genius, but to Huss was given the far greater honor of sealing his testimony with his blood. The comparison brings to mind the words of Luther, spoken of Leonard Keyser, one of the first martyrs in the German Reformation. "Who am I," he said, "a wordy preacher, in comparison with this great doer?"[2] Huss was a specimen of *great doers* in God's work.

He was a national hero in his beloved Bohemia. Wars came out of his death, this infringement of the

---

[1] Quoted in Wylie, *History*, 1.166.

[2] d'Aubigné, *History*, 4.42.

rights of his people. While Huss was no proponent of earthly arms for the advance of the gospel, the purpose of providence was stunning warfare, "the God of battles himself having apparently taken into his own hands the standard of the Hussites, unfurled by the genius of victory."[1] To this day the name of John Huss is most esteemed. July 6th, 2015 was the 600th anniversary of his death and a coin was struck in the Czech Republic in his honor. Fearless in the face of tyranny and death, he is celebrated even as a citizen of this world. The very dust of the saints is gold.

THE GOOSE HAS FLOWN

Less than a month after these appearances, July 6th, 1415—his 42nd birthday—he was brought in for the final time before the council. "This day was to see the wishes of his enemies crowned, and his own sorrows terminated."[2] He was brought to the church and a sermon was delivered upon Romans 6:6, "that the body of sin might be destroyed."[3] The ingenious preacher handily applied this text to the execution of

---

[1] *John the Baptist*, 105. Wylie dedicates a chapter to the Hussite wars and to the fascinating martial brilliance displayed in them.

[2] Wylie, *History*, 1.161.

[3] A.V.

heretics.[1] Thirty articles of heresy were read; "the sentence coupled in closest relation Wyclif and Huss."[2] As a sampling: "the holy council, having God only before its eye, condemns John Huss to have been and to be a true, real and open heretic, the disciple not of Christ but of John Wyclif."[3] In the end, what it came to was this:

His only offense was his definition of the Church and his denial of the infallibility of the papacy and its necessity for the being of the Church. These charges constitute the content of all the 30 articles except the 25th. Luther said brusquely but truly, that Huss committed no more atrocious sin than to declare that a Roman pontiff of impious life is not the head of the Church catholic.[4]

The bishop of Lodi, who had preached the sermon, "pronounced upon Sigismund the eulogy that his name would be coupled with song and triumph for all time for his efforts to uproot schism and destroy heresy."[5] How true the prophesy, and yet how different its fulfillment from the intended

---

[1] Add another 6 to the reference and they've got their ideal verse.
[2] Schaff, *History*, 5.2.381.
[3] Ibid.
[4] Ibid., 5.2.384.
[5] Ibid., 5.2.381.

meaning. Henceforth the name Sigismund would be forever coupled with the song and triumph of truth, even through the innocent blood his reckless infidelity had spilled.

Now came the defrocking ceremony. The heretic was led to the front of the church where a stack of priestly garments lay before the altar. They clothed him with all the vestments and placed the cup in his hand, before immediately taking it from him. "I hope," he now said, "that this very day I shall drink of his cup in his own kingdom."[1] Assured of God's mercy, he testifies, "he wyl not take away the chalyce of his redemption."[2] They plucked off his vestments one by one. A scissors was then used to cut a cross into his head to mark him as disqualified from the priesthood forever. He was to be a true priest and living sacrifice now. They placed upon his head a dunce cap bearing pictures of demons and the inscription *Heresiarch*, Arch-Heretic. "Most joyfully," says its recipient, "will I wear this crown of shame for thy sake, O Jesus, who for me didst wear a crown of thorns."[3] Here is one who indeed counted the reproaches of Christ greater wealth than the treasures of this world.

---

[1] Wylie, *History*, 1.162.

[2] Foxe, *Acts*, 2.291.

[3] Wylie, *History*, 1.163.

It is not impossible that as they did this, he turned to them and said, "In 100 years you shall answer before God and before me."[1] Men on the verge of death have been known to reach nigh unto mysterious utterance. In any case, it is without doubt that John Huss forespoke, to one degree or another, the coming Reformation.

As they led him out of the church, he passed a burning pile where all his books were being consumed.[2] The author "smyled and laughed."[3] Ever carnally minded, his foes believe they can destroy the truth by burning the physical books in which it is written. Stronger writings of truth, styled by God's own hand through him, were to endure, even the hearts of living men.

As they reached the place where he was to be executed by fire, he turned from the crowd and prayed to his God. "We know not what his life has been," they say, "but verily he prays after a devout and godly fashion."[4] Schaff styles him "the preacher whose life was, by the testimony of all contemporaries, almost without a blemish."[5] Would to God that more of such blameless men illuminated our own twisted generation.

---

[1] Ibid., 1.162.

[2] Schaff, *History*, 5.2.382.

[3] Foxe, *Acts*, 2.292.

[4] Wylie, *History*, 1.164.

[5] Schaff, *History*, 5.2.375.

When they brought him to the very spot of his execution he was offered one more opportunity to recant his errors. "What errors shall I renounce? I know myself guilty of none. I call God to witness that all that I have written and preached has been with the view of rescuing souls from sin and perdition; and, therefore, most joyfully will I confirm with my blood that truth which I have written and preached."[1] His heart was thrust upon God. "I shall die with joy to-day in the faith of the Gospel which I have preached."[2] At the hearing of these words they left him to his fate, and "John Huss had now done talking with men."[3]

Roman Catholic historians who were present say that he went to the stake with more joy than if he were going to a wedding feast.[4] They took the Goose by the neck and fastened him to the stake, piling wood up to his chin. The fires were lit, but no cry of pain did he utter. He began to sing hymns unto the Lord Jesus Christ. "Have mercy on me, Son of David! Have mercy on me, Son of David!" He was full of heavenly cheerfulness in his crucible; there was Another with him in the flames, who comforted him. His soul was preserved unsinged, not only in ecstatic expectation of appearing in heaven *that very*

---

[1] Wylie, *History*, 1.164.

[2] Schaff, *History*, 5.2.382.

[3] Wylie, *History*, 1.164.

[4] Poggius and Aeneas Sylvius, ibid.

hour—who can imagine it?—but also in present fellowship with the living God-Man. As he repeated the hymn a third time, a great wind blew over the plain, driving the fire into his face and choking him out. The Lord took him, and his body hung lifeless. The Goose is cooked, and yet his soul has flown the coop. John Huss was now finally, as the saying goes, *free as a bird.*

When the fire went out they found that it had only consumed his legs. They relit in their zeal the fire to burn the heretic's body whole, cutting up his remaining parts and roasting his heart on a stick.[1] They threw in all his garments and possessions, lest any relic should remain to add fuel to the cause. When all was reduced to ashes, they dug up the ground to four feet deep, "so anxious were his persecutors that not the slightest vestige of John Huss—not even a thread of his raiment, for that too was burned along with his body—should be left upon the earth."[2]

They dropped all the remains into the Rhine and wiped their hands, unable, however, to remove the red. It was their own defeat which they had sealed; they had "set an ambush for their own lives."[3] "When the martyr bowed his head at the stake it was

[1] Foxe, *Acts*, 2.293.
[2] Wylie, *History*, 1.164.
[3] Prov. 1:18.

the *infallible* Council that was vanquished. It was with Huss that the victory remained and what a victory! Heap together all the trophies of Alexander and of Caesar, what are they all when weighed in the balance against this one glorious achievement?"[1] Were they to have devised a way to steel the movement with maximum energy, they could not have landed on a more expedient course than that which they had actually followed with Huss. "From the moment he expired amid the flames, his name became a power."[2] The Fathers of the Council had sneered, "If the master burns, there is likely to be warm work with the disciples."[3] Warm work it was to be indeed, even unto the promised fiery tongues of the Holy Spirit!

> "Huss is dead," say they, as they retire from the meadow where they have just seen him expire. Huss is dead... No: Huss is alive. It is not death, but life, that he has found in the fire; his stake has given him not an entombment, but a resurrection. The winds as they blow over Constance are wafting the spirit of the confessor and martyr to all the countries of Christendom. The nations are being stirred; Bohemia is awakening.[4]

---

[1] Wylie, *History*, 1.164-65.

[2] Ibid., 1.165.

[3] *John the Baptist*, 82.

[4] Wylie, *History*, 1.165.

One hundred years pass, and if you were in the right place, at the right time, you would perhaps spy an unassuming yet determined figure moving through the crowd and, shortly thereafter, hear mighty strokes of a hammer falling against a Wittenberg church door. The hour has struck; all of Christendom is being called to a reckoning.

PEACE TO THY MEMORY—THOU NOBLE, FAITHFUL HUSS![1]

---

[1] *John the Baptist*, 106.

Made in the USA
Las Vegas, NV
15 July 2021

26515697R00035